RACISM

Changing Attitudes 1900-2000

R. G. Grant

RSVP
RAINTREE
STECK-VAUGHN
PUBLISHERS
A Steck-Vaughn Company

Austin, Texas

TWENTIETH CENTURY ISSUES SERIES

Censorship
Crime and Punishment
Medical Ethics
Poverty
Racism
Women's Rights

Published by Raintree Steck-Vaughn Publishers,
an imprint of Steck-Vaughn Company

Library of Congress Cataloging-in-Publication Data
Grant, R. G.
Racism / R. G. Grant.
     p.   cm.—(20th Century Issues)
     Includes bibliographical references and index.
     Summary: Discusses racist attitudes of white people in the twentieth century, how Africans and Asians have struggled against this racism, and changes in European and North American attitudes to include a vision of multiracial future.
     ISBN 0-8172-5567-2
     1. Racism—Juvenile literature.
     [1. Racism. 2. Prejudices.]
     I. Title. II. Series.
     HT1521.G677 1999
     305.8—dc21   98-49102

Printed in Italy. Bound in the United States.
1 2 3 4 5 6 7 8 9 0 04 03 02 01 00

Picture acknowledgments
Amnesty International 18; Associated Press 39, 41, 43; Associated Press/Topham 4, 51, 55, 58; Camera Press 52; Corbis-Bettmann/Reuter 50; Corbis-Bettman/UPI 37, 40, 47; Mary Evans Picture Library 5, 6, 8, 11, 12, 13, 14, 20, 21, 22, 27, 28; David Hoffman 53 (bottom), 57; Hulton Getty Picture Collection 9, 15, 16, 30, 32, 49; Impact 45 (E Andrews), 48 (Rhonda Klevansky), 56 (Billy Paddock); Popperfoto 17, 23, 31, 35, 42; SIPA-Press 54; Tony Stone Images 59 (John Fortunato); Topham Picturepoint 29, 36, 44, 46; UPI/Corbis 25, 38; Wayland Picture Library 7, 18, 33, 34, 53 (top).

Cover: main picture shows skinheads giving the Nazi salute during a racist demonstration in Germany (SIPA-Press); black-and-white pictures show, top to bottom, Jewish families being rounded up by German soldiers during World War II (Wayland Picture Library); separate facilities for Europeans in India under British rule (Topham Picturepoint); and white racists demonstrating during a civil rights protest in Chicago, 1966 (Topham Picturepoint).

CONTENTS

A RACIST WORLD

OPINION

In 1839, the naturalist Charles Darwin wrote: "When two races of men meet, they act precisely like two species of animals. They fight, eat each other..."

German racists demonstrate against the presence of immigrants and asylum seekers in their country.

At recurrent intervals throughout history, human beings have tended to despise and dislike people they see as different from themselves. The difference might be one of language, religion, or social class. It might be a matter of physical characteristics, such as skin color. Or it might simply be a question of wearing a different style of clothing or supporting a different sports team.

Racism grows out of this hostility to, or contempt for, people who are "different." Racists believe that a person's character and abilities are determined by the physical group to which they are thought to belong. And, since a person cannot change the physical group he or she was born into, racism allows no possibility of escape through education or individual self-improvement.

Racists believe that their own culture or people is superior to others. They consequently feel justified in treating members of other ethnic groups as inferiors and may make them targets of hatred, abuse, and discrimination. Racism affects societies in a range of practical ways—people may be denied educational opportunities and jobs and suffer the day-to-day humiliation of being regarded as different and inferior. In the most extreme cases, people are sometimes systematically killed because of their supposed race.

This book is mostly about the racist attitudes of Europeans and people of European origin—"white" people—in the twentieth century, and about how other peoples, such as Africans and Asians, have struggled against this racism.

Of course, white people have not been the only people in history to feel racial superiority—far from it. For example, Arabs had a long tradition of using

This nineteenth-century engraving shows black captives being taken for sale by Muslim slave traders in East Africa.

black slaves, which they justified by seeing Africans as inferior beings. Some African peoples felt superior to other African peoples and dominated and exploited them. Some Japanese still believe that they belong to a naturally superior race and look down on other Asians, especially the Koreans.

Nevertheless, white racism has been one of the central issues of twentieth-century life. It has been the focus of political struggles and personal battles that have helped shape the century. This book charts the changes in European and North American attitudes toward race in the twentieth century—and sees how a vision of a multiracial future has grown from the struggle against white dominance and prejudice.

WHITE SUPREMACY

At the start of the twentieth century, most white people regarded themselves as superior to all other ethnic groups. To almost any white person, it seemed obvious that Africans, Arabs, Asians, and Native Americans were inferior peoples. This sense of

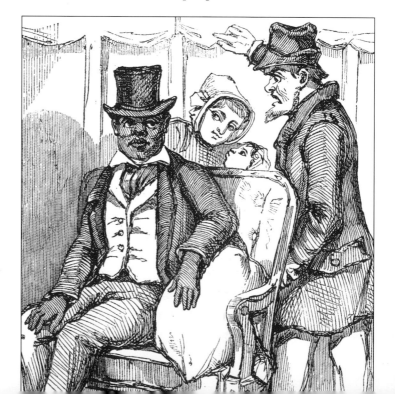

This cartoon, published in 1856, shows a white American insisting that a black passenger should leave his seat in a railroad car used by whites.

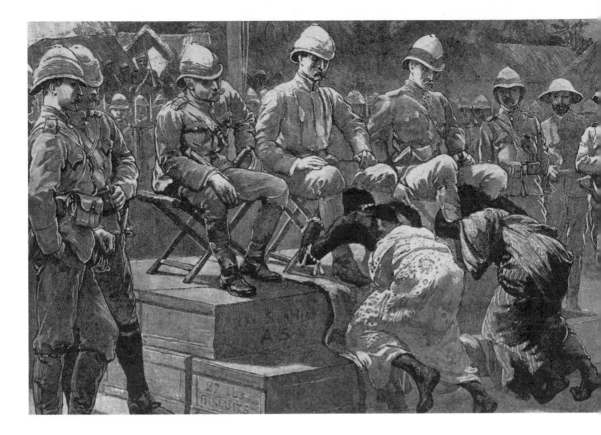

superiority was based on the extraordinary dominance that whites had achieved across the world. By 1900, they had taken direct political control of most of the planet. Their progress in warfare, science, and technology—from the steam engine to the machine gun—had given them a power and wealth that no other people could match.

In 1896, the Ashanti people of West Africa were defeated by the British. Their ruler, King Prempeh, was forced publicly to kiss the feet of his white conquerors.

As well as exercising direct rule over their colonies, the Western powers treated independent states ruled by nonwhites with general contempt. For example, China was officially independent, but Europe and the United States ran areas of the country, known as "concessions," and behaved toward the Chinese with utter disrespect. White people were not subject to Chinese law and always took precedence over the Chinese, for example, in a line for a train ticket. Only Japan had won a grudging respect by building up a modern military force that could take on the Europeans.

As this cartoon suggests, the naturalist Charles Darwin revealed that human beings evolved from apes. Some nineteenth-century scientists claimed that the "inferior races" were closer to their ape ancestors.

SCIENTIFIC RACISM

Science had given its backing to the idea that white dominance over the other peoples of the earth was natural and justified. In his book *The Origin of Species*, published in 1859, the naturalist Charles Darwin had explained evolution as the "survival of the fittest." This idea was seized on by thinkers known as "Social Darwinists" to explain white supremacy. Because the white race was fitter to survive, they said, it rightly dominated and exploited less fit races.

Nineteenth-century European and American anthropologists studied differences in human physical characteristics in order to classify people by race. By measuring skulls, they claimed to be able to place the different races in line of evolution from our ape ancestors. Conveniently, they concluded that "Caucasian" whites were furthest evolved from the apes, and "Negroes" were closest to humans' animal origins.

Other anthropologists who studied human cultures, rather than bodies, classified races in terms of historical progress. They concluded, unsurprisingly, that whites had progressed the furthest. They had created "advanced civilization," whereas blacks were, on the whole, living the most "primitive" lives. The Asiatics were somewhere in between. In the 1890s, a German-born American anthropologist, Franz Boas, began to argue that societies and races were not more or less "primitive" or "advanced." They were simply different. But it would be a long time before this idea, known as "cultural relativism," won acceptance.

RACISM AND RIGHTS

By 1900, scientific racism had developed into an elaborate system that placed all humans in a hierarchy. Yet Westerners in 1900 were also aware of quite different ways of thinking about the relations between people. Democrats, liberals, and socialists thought in terms of human rights, human equality, and universal brotherhood. Their ideas suggested that individuals should be free and equal, irrespective of race, color, or creed. Christianity also taught that every human being had a soul equally valuable to God.

Christian and liberal ideas had helped lead to the abolition of slavery during the nineteenth century (although Christian individuals and institutions had previously tolerated slavery). By 1900, all Western societies had also given full citizenship to Jews after centuries of discrimination. Many of the people who struggled against white supremacy during the twentieth century were to use the Western idea of human rights and the ideals of Christianity to counter racism.

KEY MOMENT

Science disowns racism
By the middle of the twentieth century, most scientists had stopped believing in the innate superiority of some races. This view was made official policy by the international organization UNESCO in 1945. A scientific committee set up by UNESCO to investigate racial differences concluded that "available scientific evidence provides no basis for believing that the groups of mankind differ in their innate capacity for intellectual and emotional development."

African slaves in chains in the late nineteenth century. Racist ideas were used as a justification of the slave trade.

COLONIALISM

In the early twentieth century, most Africans and West Indians and many millions of Asians were under the direct rule of the European powers. Great Britain had the largest empire, but France, the Netherlands, Germany, Spain, Portugal, and Belgium all had substantial colonies as well. These colonies were the result of a rag-bag of conquests, wars, and treaties. Some dated back over three hundred years, but most had been acquired in the second half of the nineteenth century.

All the European colonial powers were at least to some degree democracies. In general, they acknowledged the right of people to a say in choosing their own government. But most nonwhite inhabitants of the colonies had few political rights if they had any at all. The colonial rulers justified this denial of rights and the seizure of foreign lands by claiming to be the bearers of a superior civilization. They claimed that Europeans had to govern these countries because the nonwhites were barbarians, incapable of running their own affairs. Attitudes such as these ignored the historical reality of ancient and advanced Chinese, Indian, and African civilizations.

School books, popular newspapers, and novels in European countries promoted empire by depicting African and Asian peoples as childlike, grateful subjects, or as savages to be rightfully gunned down. Stereotypes such as the mysterious, sinister Oriental and the fierce African cannibal were the stuff of all European children's literature. The "exotic" cultures of the colonized peoples were an object of superior curiosity to educated Europeans. Western artists reveled in the "primitivism" of African and Polynesian masks.

This French newspaper of 1911 shows France as the bringer of civilization to a benighted North Africa.

The Amritsar massacre
Amritsar is a city in the Punjab, in northern India. In April 1919 it was the site of riots as agitation for Indian self-government mounted. On April 13, troops led by the local British commander, General Dyer, fired on a crowd of Indian men, women, and children in a public park. In all, 379 people were killed and close to 1,200 were injured. The massacre convinced many Indians that only complete independence from Great Britain could bring just and humane rule to the subcontinent.

SEGREGATION AND MIXING

In practice, forms of racial segregation existed in all colonial societies. Whites lived separate lives to which other races generally had access only as servants or as specially privileged guests. In countries such as Kenya and South Africa, other races were also segregated. Indians brought there to serve the needs of the British Empire were treated as a class "above" the blacks but "below" the whites.

However, the Europeans could not run their empires without the cooperation of large numbers of local people. Locally recruited soldiers, police, and clerks were the backbone of imperial rule. At a higher level, the Europeans often gave a share in power to small minorities of nonwhites whom they saw as racially

European colonists like to represent themselves as educators rather than oppressors. This illustration shows a French colonial official teaching improved agricultural techniques to farmers in Madagascar—a country where the French, in fact, carried out appalling massacres.

and culturally superior to other non-whites. In French colonies, a policy of "assimilation" sought to create a privileged minority of leaders that would be French by culture and influence even if of a different race. The British preferred to make alliances with traditional local rulers, such as the maharajas of India and the Muslim princes of West Africa.

Some nonwhites in the colonies came to be treated almost as honorary whites. Well-off Indians sent their children to British private schools—Jawarhalal Nehru, the first leader of independent India in 1947, was educated at Harrow, the same school attended by Great Britain's famous prime minister, Winston Churchill. The Indian prince K. S. Ranjitsinjhi, who went to Cambridge University, played cricket for Sussex and England. A hero of many English schoolboys, he topped the county batting averages in 1900.

The adoption of cricket in India and the West Indies—the first West Indian cricket team toured England in 1900—is a reminder that the subject peoples in the colonial empires sometimes willingly adopted aspects of the culture of their European masters. Many eagerly sought European-style education, which offered a path to jobs and business opportunities in the colonial world. The Christian religion, brought by missionaries, was taken up with enthusiasm by many Africans. And European ideas of democracy, nationalism, and human rights were adopted by nonwhites for use as a weapon against the colonial authorities.

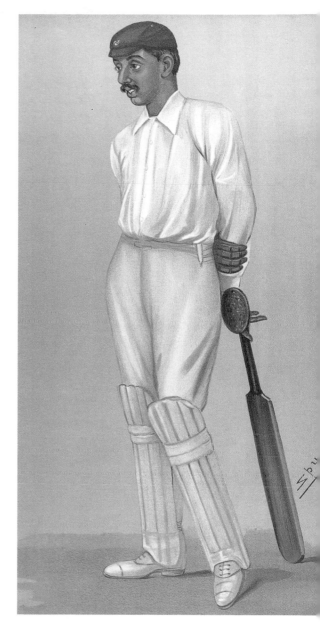

The Indian prince Ranjitsinjhi was a leading cricketer in England in the early twentieth century. Indian aristocrats who had been educated in Britain were accepted by, and mixed with, the British aristocracy on more or less equal terms.

TOWARD INDEPENDENCE

The idea that the European colonies might some day become independent states gathered ground through the early decades of the century. At the end of World War I—a struggle in which almost a million Indian soldiers fought for Great Britain—the British government publicly committed itself to granting self-government to India at some unspecified time in the future. When Great Britain took over some territories from the defeated German and Ottoman empires, it held them as a "trustee"—to rule until the local people were fit to rule themselves. However, this was not expected to happen for a very long time indeed.

A propaganda image from World War I celebrates the support Indian troops were giving to British soldiers on the Western Front. Many Indians felt they should receive self-rule in return for their contribution to the war effort.

India will help.
L'Inde aidera.

PATRIOTIC
1047

The colonized peoples were not prepared to wait passively for Europeans to grant independence, however. Led mostly by men who had received European-style educations, they began to organize against colonial rule. The origin of the movement to free Africa from colonialism dates back to the Pan-African Congress of 1900, chaired by the African-American leader W. E. B. Du Bois. By the 1920s, in Great Britain's West African colonies at least, an elite of African journalists and lawyers were prepared to criticize the colonial government and resist it in the law courts. But very little progress was made toward African independence before World War II (1939–1945).

In the first half of the century, by far the most prominent independence struggle was in India. Although Great Britain was committed to progress toward self-government, Indian movements pushing for rapid progress toward self-rule—chiefly the Congress Party—met stiff and sometimes brutal resistance from the British authorities. In 1915, Mohandas (Mahatma) Gandhi, a British-trained lawyer who had led resistance to racist policies in South Africa before World War I, returned to his native India. Gandhi applied principles of nonviolent resistance and civil disobedience in a campaign opposing British rule. His ability to mobilize the Indian people made him a force to be reckoned with.

Gandhi sets out on the 1930 Salt March, part of his nonviolent campaign against British rule in India.

KEY MOMENT

The Salt March
One of the most famous events in Gandhi's campaign of civil disobedience against British rule in India was the Salt March of 1930. Gandhi wanted to protest the British tax on salt production. He led thousands of followers on a 200-mile march to the sea. There he picked up a piece of natural salt, symbolically defying British control.

OPINION

Asked what he thought of Western civilization, Gandhi is said to have replied: "Western civilization? I think it would be a good idea."

After World War II, European powers faced armed revolts in some of their colonies. These French soldiers were photographed during the battle of Dien Bien Phu, in which Vietnamese rebels inflicted a humiliating defeat on the French Army.

THE END OF COLONIALISM

The experience of World War II fundamentally undermined the European colonial empires. The European powers were fatally weakened both economically and militarily. Japanese victories in Asia in 1941 and 1942 showed that the white colonialists could be defeated by nonwhites. The Europeans were losing faith in their God-given mission to rule the other peoples of the world.

In 1947, Britain hurriedly gave independence to its Indian Empire, and the subcontinent was partitioned into India and Pakistan. In 1949, China became a Communist state and soon became a major independent power again. In southeast Asia the Dutch, faced with a growing independence movement, were forced to leave Indonesia. In Indochina (Vietnam, Cambodia, and Laos), France never fully regained the control it had had before the war. The French Army was defeated by the Communist-led Viet Minh at Dien Bien Phu in 1954. The invincibility of white power was truly at an end.

In Africa, a new generation of leaders emerged after World War II, including Kwame Nkrumah from the Gold Coast (now Ghana), Jomo Kenyatta from Kenya, and Leopold Senghor of Senegal. Initially, Great Britain and France hoped to give their African colonies a measure of self-government, but stopped

Kikuyu suspects arrested by the British colonial authorities during the Mau Mau uprising in Kenya in the 1950s.

This cartoon shows the British authorities in Kenya inviting Africans to farm the most fertile land in the country. This land had previously been reserved for white settlers.

short of full independence. Both Nkrumah and Kenyatta spent time in prison as they agitated against the colonial authorities.

Eventually, the British and French gave up the struggle, granting independence to almost all their remaining colonies between 1956 and 1965. Nkrumah cooperated with the British in guiding the Gold Coast to independence in 1957. Kenyatta became independent Kenya's first prime minister in 1963. By the mid-1960s, only Portugal still had major colonies in Africa—they became independent after a revolution in Portugal itself in 1974 and 1975.

INDEPENDENCE AND DIGNITY

Independence undoubtedly enhanced the dignity of Asians and Africans worldwide. When African ambassadors began to arrive at the UN headquarters

OPINION

In 1960, on a visit to South Africa, British prime minister Harold Macmillan voiced his reluctant acceptance of African independence: "The wind of change is blowing through the continent. Whether we like it or not, the growth of national consciousness is a political fact."

in New York in the 1960s, they were the first blacks that African Americans had ever seen in positions of power and authority.

But independence also led inevitably to a measure of disillusionment. India maintained democracy, but many of the former colonies ended up under the rule of military governments or corrupt dictatorships. Most colonies remained to a large degree economically tied to the former colonial powers, a situation of dependence sometimes known as "neo-colonialism."

Ironically, perhaps the worst legacy the new independent states took from colonialism was ethnic conflict. No longer ruled by whites, many of the new countries were dominated by one ethnic group at the expense of others. In Sri Lanka, Sinhalese ruled Tamils, who revolted against them. In Uganda and Kenya, Asians were persecuted by black African governments. In Burundi and Rwanda, Tutsi and Hutu vied for power. The decline of white power had unleashed other ethnic hatreds.

KEY MOMENT

UDI

In 1965, white settlers in southern Rhodesia revolted against the British government's plans for independence under a democratically elected government. To preserve white supremacy against the black majority of the population, the Rhodesia Front, led by Ian Smith, announced a Unilateral Declaration of Independence (UDI). The white minority continued to rule Rhodesia until the end of the 1970s, fighting an increasingly bitter war against black guerrilla movements. In 1980, the country became officially independent as Zimbabwe, under black majority rule.

In 1998, children play amid war damage in Jaffna, the chief Tamil city of Sri Lanka. Tamil rebels have fought the Sinhalese rulers of Sri Lanka for many years.

RACISM IN THE UNITED STATES

In the United States, after the end of the Civil War and in the wake of the abolition of slavery in 1865, former slaves were granted full citizenship and full political rights. Until the 1890s, they were largely able to exercise these rights, including the right to vote. A significant number of African Americans were elected to political office at state and federal level.

However, in the early twentieth century, the United States was going through an especially racist phase of its history. In the southern states, a white backlash was under way. A Supreme Court judgment of 1896 had authorized the provision of "separate but equal" facilities for different racial groups. White authorities in the South were busy enacting "Jim Crow" laws, which established racial segregation of most public facilities,

At Shelbyville, Kentucky, in 1901, twenty-three African Americans were lynched by a mob after the death of a white woman.

including transportation and education. They also brought in measures such as literacy tests for voter registration, which were applied dishonestly and unfairly to prevent African Americans from voting.

THE KU KLUX KLAN

Lynching (the execution of an accused person without lawful trial) was common in the American South. It is estimated that 1,241 black people were lynched between 1900 and 1917. The 1920s were the heyday of the racist Ku Klux Klan, with its white hoods, strange rituals, and terrifying reputation for racial violence. The Klan may have had as many as five million members at its peak, mostly in southern and western states. It was not only antiblack, but was also against Catholic and Jewish immigrants.

OPINION

Booker T. Washington, the leading African-American spokesman at the start of the century, believed that the way forward for blacks was to work to improve their lives, in spite of segregation and discrimination. "Whether he will or not," Booker T. Washington said, "a white man respects a Negro who owns a two-story brick house."

The hooded racists of the Ku Klux Klan were a powerful force in America in the 1920s. This photo shows a Klan meeting near Baltimore in 1923.

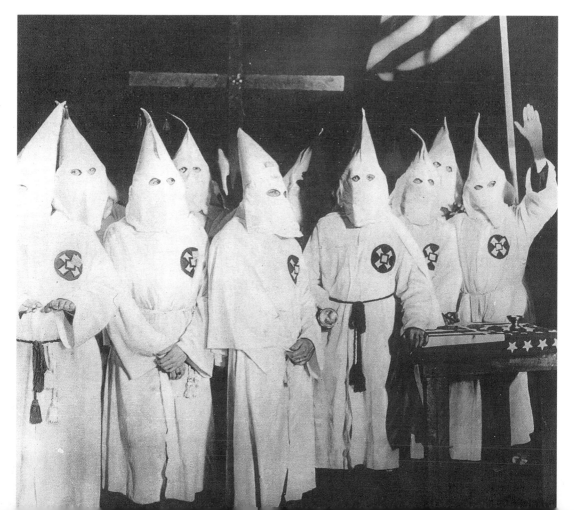

Racial criteria were increasingly applied to block immigration to the United States. American propagandists influenced by scientific racism warned of the dilution of American stock by the inferior genes of Asian, Hispanic, southern European, and Jewish immigrants. Japanese and Chinese immigration —the "Yellow Peril"—was the first to be blocked. After 1920 other groups, such as Jews, Italians, Greeks, and Poles, were kept out of the United States by immigration quotas.

ESCAPE FROM THE SOUTH

To escape the grinding poverty and racial oppression of the southern states, African-Americans moved in increasing numbers to the northern and western cities. There, in districts such as Harlem, New York, they generated a great flowering of music and other arts. Jazz, created by African-American musicians, became the favorite popular music of the Western world. But there was no escape from discrimination. At northern nightspots such as the Cotton Club, the performers were black, but blacks were not admitted as customers. Segregation was a basic fact of life in northern cities as it was in the South. African Americans lived in self-contained communities, with their own doctors and lawyers, flophouses (cheap hotels usually frequented by poor people), and bars.

The offices of the National Association for the Advancement of Colored People (NAACP) in New York in the 1930s. The NAACP works tirelessly for equal rights.

African Americans organized to fight for equality. Black academic W. E. B. Du Bois founded the Niagara movement in 1909, which would later become the National Association for the Advancement of Colored People (NAACP). Agitating for full political rights for African Americans, Du Bois' movement was the forerunner of the 1960s civil rights movement. Booker T. Washington, the other prominent African-American leader of the early part of the century, emphasized black self-help and education rather than rights.

In the 1920s, Jamaican-born Marcus Garvey encouraged black Americans to take pride in their African roots.

Both Du Bois and Washington essentially wanted an integrated society in which people would have equal opportunity, regardless of their skin color. Other African-American leaders instead praised their people's African roots and preached separate development. Marcus Garvey, a Jamaican who was prominent in the United States during the 1920s, advocated a "back to Africa" policy of subsidized black emigration from America.

KEY MOMENT

Blackface
In August 1929, NBC radio started a new comedy series, *Amos & Andy*. It featured two white actors impersonating a pair of naive southern blacks who had migrated to a northern city. The comedy turned on their hilarious ignorance and their "funny" Negro turns of phrase. Broadcast six evenings a week, this eminently racist series was the most successful radio show of the next decade.

KEY MOMENT

Concert ban
In 1939, the all-white Daughters of the American Revolution refused to allow the distinguished black opera singer Marian Anderson to perform at their concert hall in Washington, D.C. In protest at this racist prejudice, the president's wife, Eleanor Roosevelt, organized an alternative concert for the singer on the steps of the Lincoln Memorial in the center of Washington.

In 1932 at the height of the Great Depression, Franklin D. Roosevelt was elected president, promising a New Deal for the American people. Some members of his administration were actively opposed to racism, but many New Deal programs effectively accepted segregation and discrimination against blacks.

Still, many African Americans also benefited from new work opportunities, housing, and schools provided under the New Deal. There were also symbolic gestures. For example, cafeterias in government offices were desegregated, and in 1937 Roosevelt appointed the first African-American a federal court judge.

AMERICA AT WAR

The United States entered World War II in 1941, still a thoroughly racially divided society. The armed forces were strictly segregated, with blacks mostly performing menial noncombat tasks. The American attitude toward the Japanese enemy was also full of racism. People of Japanese origin in the United States were rounded up and put in prison camps in 1942, even though many were American citizens and had shown no sign of disloyalty. American wartime propaganda depicted the Japanese as subhuman, with grotesque caricaturing of their "slit eyes" and supposedly "monkeylike" features.

Still, the war brought opportunities for many African Americans. After black workers threatened to march on Washington, Roosevelt banned racial discrimination in hiring for work on federal defense contracts. Hundreds of thousands of black people moved to work in the arms factories of Detroit, Los Angeles, and Chicago. With regular work and good wages, they found a prosperity they had never known before. It would make segregation and discrimination harder to maintain after the war.

OPINION

Some black U.S. soldiers who were stationed in Great Britain during World War II were amazed at the absence of racial segregation. One lieutenant in the engineers wrote to his parents at home: "You know, the more I see of the English, the more disgusted I become with Americans. After the war, with the eager and enthusiastic support of every Negro who will have served in Europe, I shall start a movement to ship white Americans back to England and bring the English to America."

A Japanese-American family are forcibly removed from their California home in 1942. Thousands like them were shut up in internment camps during World War II.

FASCISM AND WAR

In the 1920s and 1930s, many countries, including Italy, Germany, Japan, Spain, Portugal, and Hungary, came under the rule of right-wing dictators or military governments. These regimes are often called "fascist," after the name of the ruling party in the Italian dictatorship. All the fascist rulers were extreme nationalists and militarists. They portrayed their own nation as superior to others and often used this notion to justify discrimination against minority groups or the conquest of other peoples.

The Italian dictator Benito Mussolini, who rose to power in 1922, was typical in his contempt for non-European peoples. In 1935 he invaded Africa's only fully independent state, Ethiopia. His army used poison gas and bombing to crush the resistance of Ethiopia's ruler, Haile Selassie. Japan, which came under military rule in the 1930s, invaded Manchuria in 1931 and took over much of China in 1937. The country's propagandists described the Japanese as a superior race destined to rule an Asian empire.

NAZI GERMANY

Without question, the most rabidly racist regime was the one established by the National Socialists (Nazis) in Germany. In World War I the Germans had suffered military defeat, followed by near civil war and economic chaos in the 1920s. The Nazis, headed by Adolf Hitler, claimed to have an explanation for Germany's woes. They said it was all the fault of the Jews.

Hitler had taken up some of the most extreme racial theories circulating among European writers and intellectuals at the time. He believed that the Aryans —basically, blue-eyed Germans and Scandinavians— were a naturally superior "master race." Other races, including the Slavs and Africans, were inferior *untermenschen* (underfolk), fit only to be slaves of Aryan rulers and colonists. To be great again, Hitler said, the Germans must guard their racial purity, avoiding marriage with people of non-Aryan blood. And they must crush their racial enemies, the Jews.

Hitler believed that the Slavs and Africans were inferior, but the Jews were something much worse. They were cunning conspirators whose machinations

OPINION

In his book *Mein Kampf*, published in 1925, Adolf Hitler wrote that the Nazi party "by no means believes in an equality of the races." Instead, he wrote, it believes that there is a duty "to promote the victory of the better and stronger [races] and demand the subordination of the inferior and weaker... "

German Nazi leader Adolf Hitler (right) pictured with Italian Fascist dictator Benito Mussolini

This cruel German cartoon of 1933 shows the Jews being shut out by Germany, America, France, and England. In anti-Semitic propaganda, Jews were always shown with exaggerated features supposedly representing their "racial characteristics."

were at the heart of Germany's problems. He embraced a bizarre theory, current in the 1920s, that there was a "Jewish world conspiracy." Jewish Communists in Russia and Jewish bankers in New York were said to be in league to dominate the world. Hitler saw the Jews as the embodiment of evil, determined to enslave the Aryan Germans. He said they must be got rid of, one way or another, if Germany was to be great again.

ANTI-SEMITISM

There was a long tradition of anti-Semitism (the hatred of Jews) in Europe. In areas of central and eastern Europe, such as Ukraine, Hungary, and Poland, the large Jewish communities often faced hostility from local peasants. There were large-scale massacres of Jews in the Ukraine after World War I. In Hungary in the 1920s, the ruling fascists encouraged popular prejudices against Jewish people, as well as against gypsies. Many Jews tried to leave Catholic Poland in the 1930s, feeling they were facing mounting hostility.

In North America and western Europe, including Germany, Jews were much better integrated into the wider society than were other subjects of racism. Anti-Semitic prejudice was still widespread in the early twentieth century, particularly where there were communities of new Jewish immigrants, as in London's East End. But on the whole, Jews felt they "belonged" to the countries in which they lived. In World War I, British Jews fought for Great Britain, German Jews fought for Germany, and French Jews fought for France.

In the 1920s and 1930s, fascist movements in Britain and France carried out attacks on Jews and Jewish property. Oswald Mosley, leader of the British Union of Fascists, tried to make the Jews scapegoats for Britain's problems of unemployment and economic decline. But only in Germany did anti-Semitism become the central ideology of a ruling party.

KEY MOMENT

The battle of Cable Street
In October 1936, 7,000 members of Oswald Mosley's British Union of Fascists tried to stage a march through a predominantly Jewish area of London's East End. Local Jewish people erected barricades to block the path of the black-shirted fascists. In Cable Street there was serious street fighting before the march was stopped. In the following month, the British government brought in a Public Order Act that banned political uniforms and provocative marches, effectively halting the rise of the British fascist movement.

British fascists led by Oswald Mosley hold a meeting in Trafalgar Square, London. Opponents of the fascists, in the foreground, raise clenched fists in protest.

THE RACIAL STATE

Shortly after coming to power in Germany in 1933, the Nazis imposed a one-day boycott of Jewish stores and businesses, enforced by jackbooted stormtroopers.

Hitler came to power in Germany in 1933. He set out to create the first state explicitly based on racist principles. His regime expressed a deep concern for "the purity of German blood." In 1935, Jews were banned from marriage with non-Jews, as were "gypsies, negroes, and their bastards." Committees of experts in universities and government departments devoted themselves to an exact classification of the population by race, trying to define who was or was not a Jew or a racially pure Aryan.

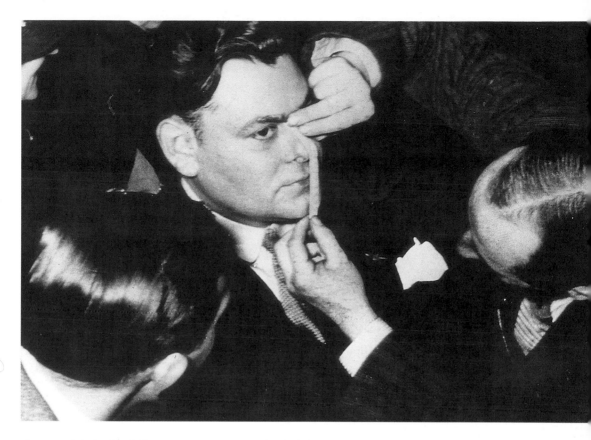

Germany's half-million Jews were excluded from most professions and subjected to a barrage of hate propaganda. Books by Jewish authors were burned, and Jewish artists were derided. By 1938, when Germany took over Austria with its substantial Jewish population, the Nazis were ready to push their anti-Semitism further. On *Krystallnacht*, November 9–10, 1938, tens of thousands of Jews were rounded up and sent to concentration camps, and Jewish businesses and synagogues were attacked and burned.

Democracies such as the United States and Britain protested at these racial attacks. But they did not generally welcome Jews who desperately sought to escape from German rule. They maintained strict policies limiting the number of Jews who could enter their countries. Britain also controlled the number of Jews going to Palestine, where Jews were working to found a homeland.

Nazi officials try to establish whether or not a person is Jewish by measuring his facial features.

OPINION

At a conference in 1938, an Australian delegate, T. W. White, explained why his government would not allow Jews fleeing Nazi rule to emigrate to Australia. "It will no doubt be appreciated," he said, "that as we have no racial problem, we are not desirous of importing one."

In 1939 Germany invaded Poland, beginning World War II. The war made it possible for Hitler to attempt to create the racial empire he had long dreamed of. By conquering the Slav countries of eastern Europe—such as Poland, the Ukraine, and Russia—the Nazis hoped to create a slave empire. The Slav *untermenschen* would provide forced labor for Aryan landowners and factory owners. Any that were not needed for work would be killed or allowed to starve to death. No Slavs would be educated, because they were only wanted for manual work. Any Slavs already educated would be exterminated.

THE HOLOCAUST

Enthusiastic young Nazis collect books for public burning. Many of them were works by Jewish authors, despised on racial grounds.

The Nazis also pursued bizarre experiments in breeding a pure master race. Children from Slav families believed to be suitable genetic material were kidnapped from their families and placed with German parents or put on farms to breed pure Aryans. Members of the SS (*Schutzstaffeln*), thought to embody the perfect genetic qualities of the master race, were encouraged to have children to create a racial elite. People thought to have defective genetic material—homosexuals, and those with mental illnesses—were marked down to be killed.

The Nazis were determined that the Jews should be got rid of entirely. By 1941, they had decided to embark on a

"cleansing" of Europe, the so-called Final Solution to the "Jewish problem." Every Jewish man, woman, and child in Europe was to be rounded up and killed. It was a project for genocide—the complete extermination of a race. Starting with massacres by firing squad in conquered areas of the Soviet Union, the Nazis progressed to the building of death camps in occupied Poland, where gas was used as a more efficient means of mass murder. This Holocaust was given the highest possible priority. Resources were even diverted from the war effort to ensure that the massacre went on.

German soldiers round up Jewish families in the Warsaw ghetto for deportation to the Nazi camps. This small boy was one of the few who survived the Holocaust.

KEY MOMENT

The Wannsee conference
In January 1942, senior German civil servants were invited to a meeting at Wannsee in the suburbs of Berlin, chaired by senior Nazi Reinhard Heydrich. They were told of the planned "Final Solution" of the Jewish problem and asked for their cooperation. The government departments agreed to help in transporting Jews to death camps from all over German-occupied Europe. Many thousands of Germans were to be involved in this massive, highly coordinated operation.

OPINION

In 1941, SS chief Heinrich Himmler told a subordinate: "The Jews are the sworn enemies of the German people and must be eradicated. Every Jew that we can lay our hands on is to be destroyed now, during the war, without exception..."

Auschwitz (Oswiecem) was the most notorious of the Nazi camps. Jews arrived there by train. On the platform they were divided into those thought useful for work and the rest—mostly women, children, the sick, and the old. These people were taken straight to changing rooms where they were ordered to undress. They were herded naked into sealed chambers and killed by poisoned gas. Their bodies were then taken by elevator to furnaces where they were burned. Most Jews arriving at Auschwitz were ashes within a few hours of their arrival.

About six million of Europe's eight million Jews died in the Holocaust. Many millions of other people—including gypsies, Poles, and Russians—also died in the Nazi camps.

The perfection of the Nazi racial empire was prevented only by defeat in World War II. Ironically, the Slav *untermenschen* of the Soviet Union proved themselves more than a match for Hitler's Aryan fighters, conquering Berlin in April 1945. Hitler died amid the ruins of his capital, still calling the destruction of the Jews his greatest work.

Jews were transported to the death camps by rail, sometimes in open train cars. Most of them were killed within hours of arriving at a camp.

RACISM DISCREDITED

Survivors of Auschwitz photographed at the camp after its liberation by Soviet troops in 1945

The Allied countries that fought against Germany, Italy, and Japan in World War II—chiefly the United States, Great Britain, and the Soviet Union—were themselves steeped in racism. Yet the horrors of Nazi rule largely discredited racism worldwide. Many Allied soldiers felt that it was one of the things they had fought against.

After World War II, most politicians hesitated to express racist ideas openly. It became simply not acceptable for scientific experts to argue that genetically transmitted characteristics made races unequal. Even the word "race" was largely dropped, being replaced by "ethnic group." Although racism of course continued, the Holocaust made it unlikely that racism on such a scale could happen again.

KEY MOMENT

The liberation of Belsen
In April 1945, the British Army liberated the Nazi camp at Belsen. They found tens of thousands of Jewish prisoners on the brink of death from starvation and disease. Emaciated corpses lay unburied in heaps around the camp. Belsen was filmed by British camera crews, and the images were shown across the world. They created an indelible impression of the horrors to which racism could lead.

CIVIL RIGHTS AND BLACK POWER

After World War II, the situation of African Americans became increasingly embarrassing to the United States government. The war had officially been fought for democracy and against racist Nazi Germany. America now claimed to be the leader of the "free world" against the threat of Communist oppression. How could segregation and the denial of rights be justified?

In the immediate postwar years, the Congress of Racial Equality (CORE) successfully campaigned to end segregation at lunch counters and other public facilities in northern cities. Segregation in sports began to crumble. In 1947, Jackie Robinson braved the racist abuse of white crowds to become the first black major-league baseball player. Althea Gibson became the first black player to break into the top levels of tennis in 1950.

In 1957, tennis star Althea Gibson became the first African American to win a Wimbledon singles title.

The United States government took some limited measures against racism. For example, the U.S. armed forces were desegregated by order of President Harry S. Truman in 1947. However, in the South, segregation and the widespread denial of civil rights remained the norm. African-American groups such as the NAACP and CORE campaigned relentlessly for full rights.

OPPOSING SEGREGATION

In 1951, Oliver Brown, an African American living in Topeka, Kansas, decided to challenge the racial segregation that prevented him sending his daughter to his neighborhood school, designated for whites only. The case ended up before the Supreme Court, where it was presented by NAACP lawyer Thurgood Marshall. In 1954, the Supreme Court ruled that racial segregation in education was unconstitutional. Whites responded by vowing to resist the racial integration of schools by force if necessary. Little more than one in fifty African-American children were attending mixed-race schools by 1964.

In the mid-1950s, a Baptist minister, Martin Luther King, Jr., emerged as an inspirational leader for the black civil rights movement. King came to prominence in 1955, when 42-year-old Rosa Parks was arrested for refusing to give up her seat to a white passenger on a bus in Montgomery, Alabama. King led a yearlong black boycott of Montgomery's bus company, which ended with the Supreme Court's outlawing bus segregation in Alabama.

Martin Luther King, Jr., delivers his famous "I have a dream" speech in Washington, D.C., in August 1963.

OPINION

One elderly woman involved in the Alabama bus boycott said: "I'm not walkin' for myself, I'm walkin' for my children and grandchildren."

Influenced by Mohandas Gandhi, King advocated nonviolent civil disobedience. In 1957, he founded the Southern Christian Leadership Conference (SCLC) and embarked on a campaign of defiance against unjust laws and regulations. His principles inspired students to begin their own campaign of "sit-ins" at segregated lunch counters and in waiting rooms and other facilities across the South. In 1960, the courage of these students, persisting in the face of violent attacks by racists and the white authorities, attracted attention worldwide.

RIDES FOR FREEDOM

The passengers on this bus were Freedom Riders protesting against racial segregation. Near Anniston, Alabama, the bus was attacked by white racists who set the vehicle on fire and assaulted the passengers.

In May 1961, CORE launched the first "freedom rides" to highlight the persistence of segregation. Two buses with integrated passengers set off on a well-publicized journey from Washington, D.C., to New Orleans. On the way, the buses were ambushed by white racists.

A Greyhound bus driver announces his refusal to drive Freedom Riders because of fears for his own safety. In the early 1960s, such fears were well founded.

Attorney General Robert Kennedy was forced to intervene in support of the riders. During the summer, more than four hundred freedom riders were arrested and three were murdered.

The spectacle of white assaults on nonviolent black protesters put the U.S. government of President John F. Kennedy under pressure to act. In August 1963, Martin Luther King led a 200,000-strong march on Washington, D.C., demanding effective civil rights legislation. The following year, Lyndon B. Johnson, who had succeeded John F. Kennedy as president, pushed through a civil rights bill that met many of the demands of the black activists. King's prestige was at its height, and he was awarded the Nobel Peace Prize.

Nonetheless, most black people in the South were still denied the most fundamental civil right, the right to vote. They were prevented from registering as voters through various legal tricks or illegal pressures. In the "Freedom Summer" campaign of 1964, several thousand students set out to register black voters in Mississippi. They met violent resistance from white racists, who did not stop short of murder.

KEY MOMENT

Sit-in at Greensboro
On February 2, 1960, four black students from North Carolina's Agricultural and Technical College in Greensboro sat at Woolworth's white-only lunch counter. In spite of insults and threats, they resolved to return every day until they were served. They were joined by other students from nearby colleges, and the sit-in movement rapidly spread to other parts of the South.

OPINION

In his emotional speech at the climax of the civil rights march on Washington, D.C., in August 1963, Martin Luther King, Jr., told the crowd: "I have a dream that my four little children will one day live in a nation where they will not be judged by the color of their skin, but by the content of their character."

President Johnson signed a voting rights act in August 1965. When it was fully enforced, this act would eventually give southern blacks the vote and undermine the white monopoly of power in the South. But the progress of civil rights legislation was slow to take effect. It also left untouched the basic issues of African-American poverty and ingrained racist attitudes.

HOSTILITY AND PREJUDICE

Hostility to African Americans was not restricted to southern white extremists. In November 1963, *Newsweek* magazine carried out a survey of white Americans' racial attitudes. It found that about one-fourth of whites objected to sharing the same lunch counter or work space with a black person. About half were upset at the idea of a black family's moving in next door to them or their child's bringing a black

Two black students carry out a "sit-in" protest at a whites-only lunch counter in North Carolina, October 1960. The waitresses won't serve them, but the students refuse to leave.

school friend over to play. And more than nine out of ten said they would object to their son's or daughter's dating an African American.

On the other side of the racial divide, by 1965 many African Americans were rejecting King's non-violence and his goal of integration in American society. King's dream had been of a "colorblind" society where people were valued for their skills and characters, irrespective of their skin color. But groups such as the Black Muslims rejected the values of white America and advocated black separatism. Malcolm X and other black nationalists abandoned King's Christian-based rhetoric of love and reconciliation. They stressed instead the need for blacks to express their anger at white racism and assert their pride in their own people. The Black Power movement, initiated by the West-Indian-born student leader Stokely Carmichael in 1966, also aggressively celebrated specifically black values.

Harassed by police dogs, civil rights demonstrators in Florida flee for safety as they are pelted with stones by white onlookers.

In the second half of the 1960s, the long-accepted term *Negro* was widely replaced by the formerly offensive "black" as a way of referring to African Americans. The belief that "black is beautiful" led some African Americans to adopt "Afro" hairstyles and clothing. They tried to break with a long-established African-American tradition of regarding a paler skin and straighter hair as more desirable than a very dark skin and curly hair. The boxer Cassius Clay joined the Black Muslims, changed his name to Muhammad Ali, and became an abrasive but dignified role model for rebellious black youths.

American medalists Tommie Smith (center) and John Carlos give the Black Power salute during the award ceremony at the 1968 Mexico Olympics.

FAILING DREAMS

Martin Luther King was assassinated in Memphis, Tennessee, in April 1968. By then, his dream of a fully racially integrated America was receding. In the cities of the north and west of the United States, a large-scale movement of white people out of city centers into new suburbs had left many African Americans trapped in poverty-stricken inner-city ghettos. Between 1964 and 1968, these areas were repeatedly torn apart by riots in which blacks fought with the police and, on occasion, the army.

The struggle for integration and equal rights continued, if in less dramatic fashion, in the 1970s. Programs such as the busing of pupils to distant schools to achieve integrated education and "affirmative action" to give blacks access to jobs and college places met strong criticism and had only

OPINION

In 1967, world boxing champion Muhammad Ali was arrested and stripped of his title for refusing to fight in America's war against the Communist Viet Cong in Vietnam. Justifying his action, Ali said: "No Viet Cong ever called me nigger."

limited success. However, many African Americans reaped the reward of the battles of the 1960s. Black politicians began to be elected to public office across the United States. In 1972, for example, Andrew Young, one of King's closest associates, became the first black congressman in the twentieth century. Schoolbooks and television programs were cleared of racist remarks. Positive images of African Americans were promoted in movies and books. The rising spending power of black consumers encouraged the making of movies and TV programs specifically targeted to a black audience.

Yet many black Americans remained trapped in a ghettoized world of poverty and crime. And many continued to believe that the United States was a white racist society in which black people would always be second-class citizens.

KEY MOMENT

Olympic salute
At the 1968 Olympic Games, held in Mexico, black American sprinters Tommie Smith and John Carlos won the gold and bronze medals in the 200 meters. During the medal ceremony, they each raised a gloved fist in the Black Power salute. This defiant gesture outraged white America, and the runners were banned from the U.S. athletics team.

OPINION

Black separatist Malcolm X completely rejected Martin Luther King's goal of an integrated America. In his view, integration was a plot to weaken blacks. "It's just like when you've got some coffee that's too black," he said, "which means it's too strong. You integrate it with cream, you make it weak."

In August 1970, Roger Mills and Berta Linson became the first mixed-race couple ever to marry in Mississippi.

APARTHEID IN SOUTH AFRICA

OPINION

An American mining engineer who went to work in South Africa in the 1930s was horrified at the treatment of black workers. His wife wrote home: "The blacks down here ... have been abused so much that they are afraid to look a white person in the face almost. But we think that blacks are a damned sight more decent than some of the whites."

Afrikaners—the Boers—with Africans at one of South Africa's earliest gold mines

At the end of the nineteenth century, South Africa was divided between areas controlled by Great Britain and areas under the rule of the Afrikaner descendants of Dutch settlers, the Boers. The defeat of the Afrikaners in the Boer War of 1899–1902 brought the whole of South Africa into the British Empire. The Union of South Africa was created as a self-governing dominion within the empire in 1910.

The Union of South Africa was ruled by the country's white minority. The black African majority did not have the vote and were systematically discriminated against. The Native Land Act, passed in 1913, banned black Africans from owning land outside areas specifically set aside for them. Another law, introduced in 1923, laid down that Africans had to have a special pass to be allowed to live in towns.

Black South Africans formed the African National Congress (ANC) in 1912 to act as a pressure group for democratic change and against racial laws. But at first the ANC had little impact.

The South African population also included a large number of Asians and people of mixed race, known as "colored." They were not treated as badly as the black Africans, but had few political rights. Mohandas Gandhi led a campaign to improve the position of Asians in South Africa before World War I.

The Afrikaners far outnumbered white South Africans of British origin, and consequently they dominated South African politics. Many Afrikaners were poor farmers or worked in relatively low-level jobs. They feared black Africans who might compete with them for land and work. Afrikaner voters increasingly backed politicians who advocated total segregation. During World War II, South Africa joined in the Allied war effort against Nazi Germany. But many Afrikaners openly admired Adolf Hitler and his racist view of the world.

Under apartheid, South African beaches were divided into separate zones for different races. This photo, taken after the ending of apartheid, shows black Africans on a beach previously reserved for "whites only."

An early protest against apartheid organized by the African National Congress (ANC) in Johannesburg in the 1950s.

OPINION

At the trial in 1964 at which he was sentenced to life imprisonment, ANC leader Nelson Mandela declared: "During my lifetime I have dedicated myself to the struggle of the African people. I have fought against white domination and I have fought against black domination. I have cherished the ideal of a democratic and free society in which all persons live together in harmony and with equal opportunities. It is an ideal I hope to live for and to achieve. But, if needs be, it is an ideal for which I am prepared to die."

After World War II, South Africa flew in the face of world opinion by embracing racist theories more thoroughly just as many other countries were being forced to abandon them. In 1948, the Afrikaner Nationalist Party won elections and began introducing the system known as "apartheid" (apartness). The aim was the complete racial segregation of South African society.

The Population Registration Act of 1950 assigned every South African to a racial category. Marriages between people in different racial categories were forbidden. Every aspect of South African life was segregated by race. There were whites-only beaches, whites-only park benches, whites-only universities, and so on. South Africa was already a racially divided and white-dominated society. Apartheid made this more complete and explicit.

South Africa's racist policies were so out of step with the times that they met with widespread condemnation. In 1961, South Africa left the British Commonwealth and became a republic. As more black African countries became independent in the

1960s, diplomatic pressure on South Africa mounted. It was expelled from the United Nations General Assembly in 1974. Boycotts stopped South Africa from taking part in international sports and cultural events.

RESISTANCE TO APARTHEID

Inside South Africa, the ANC led the resistance to apartheid. Through the 1950s, it organized a campaign of civil disobedience and protest marches. But the South African government was ruthless in suppressing opposition, using arrest without trial, torture, and even killing to crush dissent. In 1960, the ANC decided that peaceful protest alone was no longer possible, and it launched an armed struggle to overthrow the white regime.

The ANC employed a military strategy using sabotage alongside its policy of peaceful protest. But its efforts in South Africa were unsuccessful. Anti-apartheid activists had to flee the country to escape a clamp-down by the white authorities. ANC leader Nelson Mandela was sentenced to life imprisonment. Even in exile, some anti-apartheid fighters were pursued by South African agents and killed.

> **KEY MOMENT**
>
> **The Sharpeville massacre**
> On March 21, 1960, South African police opened fire on a crowd of black demonstrators protesting against apartheid laws. The police killed 69 protesters and wounded another 180. In the wake of this massacre, the South African government banned the ANC, which responded by adopting a military strategy against apartheid.

South African police stride around the bodies of black demonstrators massacred in the township of Sharpeville in March 1960.

This house is in the Kwanasha township in Natal. Under the apartheid system, black South Africans were forced to live in "townships," which had much poorer facilities than white-inhabited districts.

KEY MOMENT

Soweto riots

In the summer of 1976, black children in the Johannesburg township of Soweto walked out of school after the education authority ordered a half of all classes to be conducted in Afrikaans. Black South Africans regarded Afrikaans as the language of oppression, since it was the native tongue of the white originators of apartheid. Rioting broke out and several hundred people were killed—many of them children—as the security forces struggled to regain control.

Black resistance to oppressive white rule could not be stopped, however. It was constantly refueled by resentment at the hardships and injustices of everyday life in South Africa. Blacks who moved to the cities in search of work had to live in overcrowded townships with few facilities. Often they were forced to settle as "squatters" on land designated for whites only. This meant the authorities could at any time decide to clear them out, demolishing their homes with bulldozers. Life was, if anything, even harsher in the "Bantustans"—homelands in remote rural areas assigned to black Africans by the white government.

APARTHEID ON THE DEFENSIVE

In 1976, young blacks in the Johannesburg township of Soweto rioted against the South African education policy. This episode revealed the failure of apartheid to offer a viable future for South Africa. The white regime could stay in place only by constant police oppression. Around South Africa's borders, white rule was coming to an end, with the Portuguese colonialists quitting Angola and Mozambique in 1975, and black majority rule in Rhodesia, renamed Zimbabwe, in 1980.

White rule in South Africa was also threatened by a long-term change in the country's population. In 1911, one out of four South Africans was white. By the end of the twentieth century, whites would make up only one-tenth of the South African population.

In the 1980s, rioting in the black townships was accompanied by mounting economic pressure (sanctions) on the South African government to reform. Powerful multinational companies started withdrawing from South Africa, afraid that association with racism would spoil their public image. Many Afrikaners had become much wealthier since the start of apartheid. They began to think that political reform might offer a better guarantee of future prosperity than continued segregation.

Protesters fight with police in the township of Soweto, Johannesburg, in June 1976. The black revolt in Soweto left more than a hundred people dead and shook the apartheid state.

A NEW ERA

In 1990, South African President F. W. de Klerk accepted that apartheid could not continue. He took the dramatic step of releasing Nelson Mandela from prison. The ban on the ANC was lifted, and most segregation laws were soon repealed. Finally, de Klerk agreed to full democratic elections.

ANC leader Nelson Mandela with his (then) wife Winnie after his release from prison in February 1990. Mandela had spent more than twenty-five years in jail.

At this time, there was a serious danger that South Africa would disintegrate into violent conflict. The white government had encouraged black Africans to fight one another by secretly backing the Zulu Inkatha Freedom Party in a violent conflict with the ANC in the townships. White extremists were threatening an armed struggle to maintain white supremacy. But Mandela's personality had an extraordinary impact on South Africa. He convinced white South Africans that democracy would produce a country in which all races could live together, rather than a black government bent on revenge against their white oppressors. And he managed to keep the Zulu leaders from boycotting the electoral process.

South Africa's first multiracial, democratic elections were held in April 1994, producing a massive victory for the ANC. Mandela became South Africa's first black president. A coalition government was set up, including de Klerk and Zulu Inkatha leader Gatsha Buthelezi. No one was tempted to underrate the massive difficulties faced by the new South Africa. There were no instant solutions to poverty and inequality. Crime and corruption blighted South African life. A Truth and Reconciliation Commission, headed by Archbishop Desmond Tutu, was given the task of investigating the crimes committed under apartheid, in the hope that the ghosts of the country's past could be exorcised.

South African women line up to vote in the country's first multiracial democratic elections.

Whatever the difficulties encountered, the example of Nelson Mandela's dignity, intelligence, and humanity shone out to the whole world. Like Martin Luther King, Jr., before him, Mandela was living proof that the insults heaped on black people by racists through the centuries were based on ignorance and malice.

IMMIGRATION IN EUROPE

Asians expelled from Uganda by dictator Idi Amin arrive in England in September 1972.

Until World War II, Great Britain and other European societies were overwhelmingly white societies, with only tiny minorities of people of Asian or African origin. In the 1950s and 1960s, however, the economies of Western Europe boomed, creating many more jobs than could be filled by the local European workforce. By the mid-1960s, about a million immigrants from the West Indies, the Indian subcontinent, and Africa had come to Great Britain, but entry was then sharply slowed down by immigration controls. Immigration from outside Western Europe into continental countries continued through the 1960s and 1970s, the largest group being Turks, followed by Algerians, Moroccans, and others. Some of these immigrants came as temporary workers, sending money back to their families who stayed in their country of origin, but many others settled permanently in Europe.

As the numbers of immigrants rose, so did the hostility of many white people. This was especially true of whites living in areas of cities that were transformed by large concentrations of immigrant families. They complained that immigrants were taking jobs, houses, and places in schools that should have gone to their "own kind." They also expressed crude hostility to alien foods, customs, and skin color.

KEY MOMENT

Notting Hill riots

In August 1958, there was a violent race riot in Notting Hill, London, where a large black community had built up over the previous decade. White racists provoked skirmishes in which gasoline bombs were thrown, and several people were seriously injured. The riots made race relations a headline issue in Great Britain for the first time.

Tempers flare during a confrontation between West Indians and white racists in Notting Hill, London, in 1958.

In Great Britain, for example, immigrants faced a barrage of discrimination and abuse on the grounds of their color. White landlords would often refuse to rent rooms to nonwhites, and white employers would refuse to give them jobs for which they were fully qualified. A survey in the early 1960s suggested that one out of five white British people did not want to have a West Indian co-worker, and four out of five objected to the idea of a West Indian son-in-law.

WHITE FEARS

At first, British governments broadly welcomed immigration. All people from the British Commonwealth had the right to enter Britain freely and live there permanently if they so chose. Soon, however, Conservative politicians began to worry about the effect of immigrants on Britain's national identity. Winston Churchill, prime minister in 1955, advocated using "Keep Britain White" as an election slogan. Even Labor politicians soon began to reflect white workers' concerns about immigration.

KEY MOMENT

Rivers of blood

On April 20, 1968, Enoch Powell, a Conservative politician, delivered a sensational speech in Birmingham, England, denouncing nonwhite immigration. Powell said that immigration would lead to violent conflict. Using a classical quotation, he declared: "Like the Roman, I seem to see 'The River Tiber flowing with much blood.'" Powell was dismissed from his position, but there were demonstrations in his favor by longshoremen and other groups of workers. A Gallup opinion poll suggested that 75 percent of the British people shared Powell's fears about immigration.

OPINION

A member of the National Front, interviewed in the 1970s, said: "I don't want to be with black people, I don't want a multiracial country... I want to be able to go into a pub, I want to be able to go to work without seeing a black face. The National Front is saying the sort of things I want to hear."

This house in East London has been daubed with racist graffiti to keep an Asian family from moving in.

KEY MOMENT

Neo-Nazi attacks

In the 1980s and 1990s, Europe witnessed numerous scenes of racial violence. In the summer of 1989 a South African refugee, Jerry Maslo, was murdered in Villa Literno, a small town north of Naples, Italy. In France, in 1990, a Jewish cemetery in Carpentras was desecrated with daubed swastikas, and a man's body was dug up and mutilated. In August 1992, a mob of thugs, including neo-Nazis, attacked an asylum-seekers' hostel in Rostock, Germany, while a large crowd of local people stood by and cheered. Three months later, three people were killed in the small town of Mölln when neo-Nazi skinheads attacked Turkish immigrant families and set their houses on fire.

In 1962, Britain's Conservative government passed an immigration act that restricted the number of Asians, West Indians, and Africans who could enter Britain in a given year—people from white areas of the Commonwealth were, in practice, not subject to the restrictions. Immigration was further limited by Labor governments in 1965 and 1968. But Labor also passed laws against racial discrimination and abuse. Race Relations Acts passed in 1965, 1968, and 1976 gradually extended laws against discrimination, at first, in public places and then, in the provision of jobs, housing, education, and any goods or services.

RACISM UNDERGROUND

Despite the limits set on immigration, major political parties in Western Europe would not espouse racism, partly because it was too closely identified with the discredited policies of the Nazis. It was left to extreme right-wing fringe parties to express aggressive white racism. In Great Britain, the National Front was created in 1966. In the 1970s, it looked as if the NF might become a force in British politics. In the end, however, it remained a fringe party.

In France, on the other hand, the National Front was a major electoral force by the 1990s. It reflected strong

German skinheads give the Nazi salute during a racist demonstration in Bayreuth.

racist and anti-immigrant sentiment, especially in southern France. In Germany, neo-Nazi groups also flourished in the 1990s, carrying out attacks on immigrant hostels and on individual guest-workers. The success of racist parties in both these areas was tied to high unemployment, which made repatriation of immigrants seem like economic sense and created a pool of resentful, frustrated, unemployed whites. In Germany, however, neo-Nazi activity was much more strongly opposed by mainstream politicians and antiracists than was extreme right-wing activity in France.

Immigrants lived at constant risk of violent racist attacks, either organized by extreme-right groups or carried out by white youth gangs on their own initiative. They generally received only limited help from police forces that were themselves heavily imbued with racist attitudes. In Britain in the early 1980s, there were a number of riots sparked by heavy-handed policing in immigrant areas.

Antiracists in Magdeburg, Germany, protest against the rising number of racial attacks in their country.

OPINION

A report on the London Metropolitan Police, published in 1983, concluded: "Police officers tend to make a crude equation between crime and black people, to assume that suspects are black..."

INTEGRATION

Despite racial prejudice, however, nonwhites put down roots in Europe. Blacks triumphed over racism in sports. In British soccer, for instance, black soccer players established themselves despite a torrent of racial abuse from the stands, and some became regular members of the England team. On British television, nonwhites were rarely seen in the 1960s. Some comedy programs were packed with racist jokes. By the 1980s, blacks and Asians had begun to appear as news broadcasters or in other authority roles. Multiracialism was making hesitant, uneven progress in Europe, with antiracists continually demanding change.

OPINION

A Palestinian student described how he was repeatedly abused by racist youths when he briefly visited former East Germany. They shouted: "Go home, you bastard, you're taking our jobs! We'll kill you if you don't get out quick!"

SUCCESSES AND FAILURES

KEY MOMENT

China and the West

In 1900, the European powers and the United States sent armed forces into China to crush an anti-foreigner rebellion, the Boxer uprising. China was forced to pay a massive indemnity (fine) to compensate for damage to foreigners' property. In the 1990s, even the United States, the world's greatest power, hesitated to criticize the Chinese government over human rights, fearing that American businesses might be thrown out of China.

This mixed-race couple are South African. Until very recently, their relationship would have been illegal.

The 1990s witnessed events unthinkable at the start of the century—or even fifty years ago. In 1991, American forces went to war in the Persian Gulf with West Indian-born Colin Powell as their commander-in-chief. In 1996, Koffi Annan, from Ghana in West Africa, was chosen to head the United Nations, the world's most powerful international organization. In 1997, a golfer of very mixed racial origins, Tiger Woods, won the U.S. Masters golf tournament on a course at Augusta, Georgia, where twenty years before he would not have been allowed to set foot except as a caddie.

Meanwhile, European countries scrambled to attract investment from Asia. Whereas in 1900, millions of Asians had worked for European and American colonialists, in the 1990s many British and American workers found themselves employed in factories owned by Japanese and Korean businesses. In many areas of technology, Asian countries led the way and Europe and North America struggled to keep pace.

CHANGING ATTITUDES

White attitudes about race have undoubtedly shifted considerably. One study carefully compared racial attitudes among whites in the United States in 1985 with attitudes in the 1930s. It found that whereas in the 1930s a majority of whites believed a white person should be given preference over a black if both applied for the same job, in 1985 almost all whites said that white and black should be treated equally. In the 1930s almost all whites thought marriages between whites and blacks were wrong; in 1985, two out of five had no problem at all with racial intermarriage, and only one in four thought it was positively bad.

But many—perhaps most—black people remain convinced that they live in a racist world. In 1990, twenty-nine of the world's thirty-four poorest countries were African. At the end of the twentieth century, across the world, black people still found themselves mostly among the planet's poorest and most powerless people. In the multiracial society of Brazil, for example, it was still possible to guess people's place in the social hierarchy by the degree of whiteness or blackness of their skin. African Americans were no exception to this rule, remaining on the average at the bottom of American society, as they had been throughout the century.

KEY MOMENT

Los Angeles riots
More than two decades after the apparent triumph of the Civil Rights movement, the Los Angeles riots of 1992 showed how powerful racial tensions and divisions still are in the United States. The riots were provoked by the Rodney King case. King, a young African American, was driving his car when he was stopped by white Los Angeles police officers, who subsequently beat him as he lay defenseless on the ground. The incident was, by chance, captured on video. Shown on television, the video caused widespread outrage, and the policemen were arrested. However, in April 1992, an all-white jury found the officers not guilty. The verdict sparked three days of rioting on the streets of Los Angeles in which more than fifty people died.

OPINION

Black American filmmaker Spike Lee has stressed how hard it is for people of African origin to overcome the long legacy of white racism. He pointed out that "when you're told every single day for four hundred years that you're subhuman, when you rob people of their self-worth, knowledge, and history, there's nothing worse you can do."

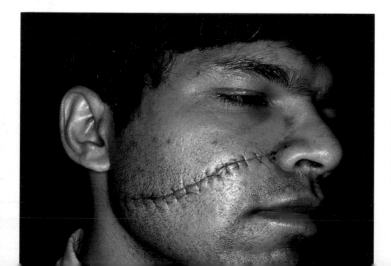

PAn Asian victim of a vicious racial attack in London

American Nation of Islam leader Louis Farrakhan addresses his followers.

Increasingly, the desire for integration expressed in the American civil rights movement has been replaced by a desire to assert a separate black identity. A prominent African-American leader of the 1990s, Louis Farrakhan, denounced white people—and especially Jews—in terms that could themselves be called racist. Black rappers such as Ice T expressed the rage and anger of members of a young generation that feels itself at war with white society. The concern with black identity has put many black activists at odds with white liberals. It has led to battles over adoption, for example, in which black activists have denounced well-meaning white people trying to adopt black children, insisting that a black child must be brought up in a black culture.

During the 1980s and 1990s, the enormous success of actors such as Bill Cosby in the United States or Lenny Henry in Great Britain could have easily created the illusion of a society in which racial problems have been solved. But even with regard to television, surveys in the United States in the 1990s showed that black and white Americans still watched substantially different programs. Predominantly white shows, such as *Friends*, that topped the U.S. viewing charts were hardly watched by black people at all.

LIMITED PROGRESS

Comparing the schoolbooks of the 1900s and those of the 1990s shows the distance covered. In the 1900s, schools explicitly taught white racial superiority and systematically stereotyped nonwhites as lazy, ignorant, and brutish. Most schoolbooks of the 1990s consciously attempted to avoid racial stereotypes; instead they sought to present racially mixed images and taught respect for other cultures and beliefs. Unfortunately, the racially integrated and harmonious world of schoolbooks—and of clothing ads—is not necessarily a mirror of the world outside.

Worldwide, ethnic tensions remain a massive force for ill. But the future will be multiracial, whether people want it or not. The different ethnic groups that populate the earth cannot be divided and put into separate "homelands." They will have to learn to live with one another. South African president Nelson Mandela called his mixed-race country the "rainbow nation," because he hoped harmony might come from diversity. In the new millennium, we need to create a "rainbow world."

KEY MOMENT

Aborigine land claims
For much of the twentieth century, Australia pursued racist policies, denying basic human rights to the Aborigines, Australia's original inhabitants. In 1993, however, the Australian Federal Parliament passed a Native Title Act. It declared that the Aborigines could, in principle, claim much of the land that was theirs before the Europeans arrived. A legal struggle is under way to determine whether Aborigines are to become major landowners in Australia.

Will children today learn to create racial harmony in the future?

GLOSSARY

anthropologist a person who studies human societies and cultures.

boycott the breaking off of trade links or other contacts with a country, as a form of protest.

Caucasian a word sometimes used, especially in the United States, for "white" people.

colony a country ruled by another country as part of its empire.

communism a system of government that promotes the view that equality and social justice can be created by a revolution abolishing private property and establishing a classless society. Communist parties have run large parts of the world during the twentieth century.

democracy a political system in which the rulers of a state are elected by the people they rule through a process of voting.

dictator a ruler who has more or less absolute power over the people he rules.

discrimination the act of treating people worse because they belong to a particular ethnic group, for example, by making it harder for them to get decent housing or jobs.

elite a group of people marked out as superior, for example, by having better education or more money than most.

ethnic group a group of people who see themselves, or are seen by others, as belonging together because they are physically similar, use the same language, or follow the same religion.

guerrilla war a war carried out by lightly armed forces that avoid full-scale battle.

guest-worker an immigrant living and working temporarily in another country.

hierarchy a system in which people are organized by rank, with those above giving orders to those below.

ideology a set of beliefs that guides people's actions.

monopoly the sole control of something, to the exclusion of everyone else.

multinational company a business that operates in many parts of the world.

multiracial involving people of different racial groups.

partitioning separating into two or more parts or countries.

propaganda the use of newspapers, television, and other media to influence people's attitudes, often employing lies and distortion.

propagandist someone who uses propaganda.

quota a fixed number or proportion.

repeal to cancel a law.

repatriation the sending back of people to what is considered to be their country of origin.

sabotage secretly destroying or damaging equipment.

segregate to make different racial groups live completely separate lives, insofar as possible, with different schools for their children, separate seating areas on public transportation, separate leisure facilities, and so on.

stereotype a widely shared notion that all members of a particular ethnic or social group have the same (usually negative) characteristic.

swastika the symbol of the Nazi Party.

townships areas of South African cities in which black people live.

BOOKS TO READ

D'Souza, Dinesh. The End of Racism. New York: The Free Press, 1996.
A highly controversial book that was denounced as racist by many African Americans. It does, however, give an excellent survey of issues such as "scientific racism" and illuminates the continuing racial divide in the United States.

Garg, Samidha and Hardy, Jan. Racism (Global Issues). Austin, TX: Raintree Steck-Vaughn, 1997.
Racial exploitation is discussed from colonial times until the present day and particular attention is given to discrimination in Europe, the United States, South Africa, and Australia.

Goldhagen, Daniel Jonah. Hitler's Willing Executioners. New York: Vintage Books, 1997.
The most controversial recent book on the Holocaust.

Grant, R. G. The Holocaust (New Perspectives). Austin, TX: Raintree Steck-Vaughn, 1998.
Described by the Times Literary Supplement as the best book for children on this topic.

Mosley, Walter. Devil in a Blue Dress. New York: Pocket Books, 1997.
One of a series of detective novels in which President Clinton's favorite author draws a vivid picture of black life in the United States since World War II.

Paton, Alan. Cry, the Beloved Country. New York: Addison-Wesley, 1998.
A much-praised novel about racism in South Africa.

Riches, William T. Martin. The Civil Rights Movement: Struggle and Resistance. New York: St. Martin's Press, 1997.
An excellent, up-to-date survey of the origins and course of the civil rights movement, and the problems it has left unresolved.

Black People in the British Empire by Peter Fryer, Pluto Classic, 1993.
An aggressively radical survey of the black experience under imperial rule.

If This is a Man by Primo Levi, Abacus, 1993.
Simply the best personal account of the Holocaust by a survivor.

Shooting an Elephant from Collected Essays by George Orwell, Penguin, 1984.
A short story that gives a gripping insight into the mentality of colonial officials.

Windrush by Michael and Trevor Philips, HarperCollins, 1998.
Accounts of the experiences of West Indians who arrived in Great Britain after World War II.

USEFUL ADDRESSES

UNITED STATES

Center for Holocaust Studies,
1609 Ave J
Brooklyn, NY 11230

Gustavus Myers Center for the Study of
Human Rights in the United States,
2582 Jimmie Avenue
Fayetteville, AR 72703

International Organization for the Elimination of
All Forms of Racial Discrimination (EAFORD)
2025 Eye Street NW, Suite 1120,
Washington, DC 20006

Martyrs Memorial and
Museum of the Holocaust,
6505 Wilshire Boulevard
Los Angeles, CA 90048

EUROPE

Amnesty International UK,
99-119 Rosebery Avenue,
London EC1R 4RE, UK

Institute of Race Relations,
2-6 Leeke Street, King's Cross Road,
London WC1, UK

SOS Racisme Internationale,
64 Rue de la Folie Mericourt, Paris 75009, France

World Council of Churches Program
to Combat Racism (WCC/PCR),
P.O. Box 2100, 150 Route de Ferney,
CH-1211, Geneva 2, Switzerland

NEW ZEALAND

Citizens Association for
Racial Equality (CARE),
P.O. Box 10.50.35, Auckland, New Zealand

INDEX

Italian people, attitudes
toward 22

Japanese Americans 24
internment of 24, **25**
Japanese people, attitudes
toward 6, 7, 16, 22, 24, 56
Jewish people, attitudes toward
9, 21, 22, 58
persecution of 26–28, **28**,
29, 30, **30**, 31–35, **31**,
33–35
"Jim Crow" laws 20
Johnson, Lyndon B. 39, 40

Kennedy, John F. 39
Kennedy, Robert 39
Kenya 12, **17**, 19
Kenyatta, Jomo 17–18
Kikuyu people 17, **17**
King, Jr., Martin Luther 37–39,
37, 40–43, 51
King, Rodney 57
Krystallnacht 31
Ku Klux Klan 20–21, **21**

Lee, Spike 57
lynching **20**, 21, 37

Macmillan, Harold 18
Madagascar **12**
Mandela, Nelson 46–47,
50–51, **50**, 59
Malcolm X 41, 43
Marshall, Thurgood 37
"Mau Mau" uprising 17, **17**
mixed-race marriage **43**, **56**, 57
Mosley, Oswald 29, **29**
Mussolini, Benito 26, **27**

National Association for the
Advancement of Colored
People (NAACP) **22**, 23, 37
National Front 53, 54
National Socialists 26, **27**, **30**,
31, 32, **32**, 33–35, 36, 45,
54
National Urban League 58
Native Americans 5, 6
Native Land Act 44

Native Title Act 59
Nazis see National Socialists
Nehru, Jawarhalal 13
neo-colonialism 19
neo-Nazis 54, **54**, 55
Niagara movement 23
Nkrumah, Kwame 17–18
non-violent resistance 15, **15**,
38, 47

Origin of Species, The 8

Pan-African Congress 14
Parks, Rosa 37
Polish people, attitudes toward
22, 34
Population Registration Act 46
Powell, Colin 56
Powell, Enoch 53
Prempeh, King **7**
*Protocols of the Elders of Zion,
The* 26

Race Relations Acts 54
race riots 22, 42, 48–49, **49**,
53, 55, 57
racial attacks 31, 53, **53**, 55, **57**
equality 6
desegregation 24, 37
discrimination 5, 9, 21, 24,
26, 44–45, 53–54
integration 23, 41, 42, 43,
58, 59
segregation 12, 20–21,
22–25, 36–38, 46, 49
Ranjitsinjhi, K. S. 13, **13**
Rhodesia 19, 48
Robinson, Jackie 36
Roosevelt, Eleanor 23
Roosevelt, Franklin D. 24
Rwanda 19

Salt March, The, 15, **15**
scientific racism 8–9, 22, 35
Selassie, Haile 26
Senghor, Leopold 17
separatism 23, 41, 58
Sharpeville massacre 47, **47**
Sinhalese people 19
sit-ins 38–39, **40**

Slav people 27, 32, 34
slavery **5**, 6, **9**
abolition of 9, 20
Smith, Tommie 43
Social Darwinists 8
South Africa 12, 15, 44–51, 56
sanctions against 49
Southern Christian Leadership
Conference (SCLC) 38
Sri Lanka 19, **19**

Tamil people 19, **19**
Till, Emmet 36
townships 48, **48**, 49
Truman, Harry S. 37
Tutu, Archbishop Desmond 51

Uganda 19, **52**
UNESCO 9
United Nations 6, 18, 47, 56, 58
Universal Declaration of
Human Rights 58

Viet Minh 17
Vietnam **16**, 17
Dien Bien Phu **16**, 17

Wannsee conference 33
Warsaw ghetto **33**
Washington, Booker T. 21, 23
West Indies 10, 13, 52
Jamaican revolt 16
white supremacy 6, 8, 9, 19, 59
Woods, Tiger 56
World War I 6, 14, **14**, 15, 26,
28, 29, 45
and Indian soldiers 14, **14**
World War II 14, 16, 17,
24–25, 32, 34–35, 36, 45,
46, 52, 58

"Yellow Peril" 22, 24
Young, Andrew 43

Zimbabwe 19, 48
Zulu Inkatha Freedom Party
50–51